BEEHAVER OR BEEKEEPER

DEWEY MASSEY

CONTENTS

1

THE ART OF BEEKEEPING

void anyone that tells you that their way is the only way.

BEE KEEPING IS NOT for everyone even though everyone thinks they are a Beekeeper. Being a Beekeeper is very complicated, time consuming and expensive! Just because you have bees, it does not make you a BeeKeeper!

LEARN TO BECOME A DIY BEEKEEPER, making your own boxes and other supplies. Work with others as a group to save money and freely share ideas. Help one another graduate from BeeHavers to BeeKeepers!

THERE IS no one that has the answers to everything. What works for your neighbor or buddy may not work for you. There is NO single correct approach to beekeeping.

. . .

One of the hardest things for even the most experienced beekeeper to do is to stop attempting to outthink the Honeybees. You must continuously be willing to learn from your bees. Try to thinking you know everything and begin to Think Like a Honeybee!! Learn to adapt as it is needed.

What color should my boxes be?

Do you think the Honeybee truly cares? What colors are the trees, rocks, walls, tires, trailers, water meter bases, apartments, homes, churches and other cracks and crevices do they build their homes in?

Which direction should I face my hives?

Go out into the wild to see which direction the Honeybees choose. You will find them facing a multitude of directions.

How high should my hives / swarm traps be off the ground?

How high in the trees, rocks, walls, tires, trailers, water meter bases, apartments, homes, churches and other cracks and crevices do they build their homes in? Hint: Make them at the height that is most comfortable for you!!

There are many more questions that can be answered by just taking the time to consider what would the Honeybees do!

~

THOUGH THERE IS no one answer to a simple beekeeping question. Each person that gives an answer may differ slightly. You must be willing to share what you have learned as well as be willing to learn from other beekeepers but be willing to adapt as the need arises.

I AM TELLING no one to join any Beekeeping Club but you would best be served to gather a group of beekeeping friends to share information and assist each other when it is needed.

IF YOU MUST SEEK out assistance do so by locating a beekeeper near you and spend time assisting them in their apiary. Avoid the YouTube trap as they are more interested in view counts and subscriptions that actually helping when it is really needed. Find someone that will give you a phone number so that you can actually talk to or at least text them.

First Steps prior to Keeping Bees

- Check restrictions for beekeeping in your area.
- State, County, Community, HOA may all have rules that need to be followed.
- Talk with your family, friends and neighbors before getting bees

Get them onboard before you get your honeybees!

- Are there water fountains, or swimming pools nearby?
- Are they afraid of Honeybees and/or wasps?
- Do they have a strong allergic reaction to bee stings?
- Select your hive location carefully and be understanding when others are concerned

Always be aware of people and paths.

- Select a sunny location to set up your hives
- Use fences, walls, or plants to direct your bees up!
- Make sure it has easy access and room to work on your colonies!

Things to consider before you begin to purchase a Beehive

- Is the area in a location that is Sunny & warm
- Is there a natural Wind break the protect your colonies on those cold winter nights
- Is the location in a spot where there will be early morning sun on the hive opening
- Is the location where you are easily able to access hive from sides or back

Supplies for the New Beekeeper

Not everyone will have your best interest at heart even if they are the one that is selling you your products or even Honeybees I am sure they will be thrilled to sell you as many as you may need!

Everyone has their favorite items that they will tell you that you must use. You will find that of the people you may seek advice from just happen to sell those same items that they say you must have, which may seem convenient, but you should use your own judgement.

There is an overwhelming selection of options for the beekeeper just remember what works for them may not work for you.

It does not matter what your neighbor, the Club Guru or your favorite YouTube Superstar may tell you just remember There is no one "best" solution!

You will find many willing to sell you their local products and tell you that what they offer is best but take the time to look around you will find many times the LOCAL guys are the highest even though they may not offer what is best for you. This includes gear as well as Honeybees.

Beginning Beekeeping Supplies

- Hive - *It is best that you decide this way before you get your bees.*
- Bee Jacket or Suit - *Many shapes and forms but the price you pay does not always mean it is the best*
- Veil - *Many shapes and forms but the price you pay does not always mean it is the best*
- Bee Gloves - *Use nitrile gloves instead of bulky leather gloves*
- Bee Smoker - *Multiple designs just remember simplest works best*
- Hive Tool - *Multiple designs but you can find the same item at hardware stores and possibly cheaper*
- Uncapping Tool - *Multitudes of designs but find what works best for you not really needed until your second year as a BeeKeeper*
- Brush - *Avoid as the girls will not like it use a turkey feather instead*
- Honeybees - *What breed will serve you best. Each species has their pros and cons so do the research.*

Just as mentioned prior there are many different types of gear for the new beekeeper to choose from, but we will begin with the Hive itself. There are many different types of hives being used and more developed every year and each is the best and savior of the beekeeping community. There are a few what I would call gimmick hives, supers, add-on boxes or whatever you wish to call them but those would be best thought of after you have successfully gotten your colonies through at a minimum of 2 winters.

We will concentrate our discussions on the Langstroth Hive!

One hundred and fifty years after Rev. Langstroth, from Philadelphia, invented the Langstroth hive in the mid 19th century, which revolutionized beekeeping. This beehive is still the most used type of hive in the United States.

THE LANGSTROTH DESIGN has removable frames which makes it easy to inspect your hive and maximize honey production. There are many advantages to this design. You will find that there is a multitude of other gear for the beekeeper which includes more modern automatic honey harvesting equipment which includes decapper and extractors which are specifically designed for Langstroth hive frames.

ALL IN ALL, **Langstroth hives are a great choice for beginning beekeepers.**

THE LANGSTROTH CONSISTS of a series of boxes, called **supers**, stacked on top of each other. Typically, there are deep supers (or brood boxes) and medium or shallow supers used for the girls to store honey. These supers rest on a bottom board and are topped by an inner and outer cover.

EACH BOX HOLDS removable frames where the honeybees build comb. The frames of a standard Langstroth hive will have the same length and width in all the boxes. A traditional 10 frame Langstroth box is 16" wide by 19 7/8" long and the size of the box, deep, medium, or shallow, will determine the height of the frames.

- Deep: 9 5/8"
- Medium: 6 5/8"
- Shallow: 5 7/8"

Apart from reduced weight and capacity, there is little practical difference between 8 and 10 frame Langstroth beehives. Though the 10 frame Langstroth is easily the most popular, there are other choices to be made when utilizing a Langstroth Design Honeybee Hive:

A. Ten-Frame Langstroth Hive

In a 10-frame Langstroth Hive the boxes are sized so that they will hold at the most 10 frames which the girls build their honeycomb in. The idea is the bees attach the comb to the edges of the frames, most utilize a honeycomb embossed foundation made from beeswax. This way the bees will build their honeycombs where you want. Check with one of your beekeeping friends to find out what happens when you make a mistake and leave even one frame out causing too much free space.

THE STANDARD 10 frame Langstroth supers can be extremely heavy. A ten-frame super full of honey can weigh as much as **80 pounds!**

10 Frame Langstroth Beehive Measurements

All 10 frame Langstroth Beehives have the same length and width – 19 ⅞ inches long and 16 inches wide. The difference is the depth. As you can see in the chart below, shallow, medium, and deep boxes have different depth measurements.

Type	Depth	Length	Width
Deep	9 5⁄8 inches	19 ⅞ inches	16 inches
Medium	6 5⁄8 inches	19 ⅞ inches	16 inches
Shallow	5 7/8 inches	19 ⅞ inches	16 inches

10 Frame box full of honey

- Shallow – 40 pounds
- Medium – 50 pounds
- Deep – 80 pounds

B. Eight-Frame Langstroth Hive

Eight-frame Langstroth hives use the same design as the classic ten-frame hives do. But there is one main difference. It only has eight frames instead of ten. There are pros and cons to each?

With only eight frames this means your supers are smaller and lighter. The eight frame super full of honey will weigh quite a bit less than a 10 frame super full of honey. The smaller frame count can save your back especially if you have multiple colonies to tend with.

The main downside to the eight-frame hive is that it is not as common as the ten-frame. So, parts are more difficult to find, and it's more difficult to work with other beekeepers.

8 Frame Langstroth Beehive Measurements

8 Frame Langstroth Beehive measurements are very close to the 10 frames. The width of each box is 2 inches shorter because it holds less frames.

Type	Depth	Length	Width
Deep	9 5⁄8 inches	19 7/8 inches	14 inches
Medium	6 5⁄8 inches	19 7/8 inches	14 inches
Shallow	5 7/8 inches	19 7/8 inches	14 inches

8 Frame box full of honey

- Shallow – 32 pounds
- Medium – 40 pounds
- Deep – 64 pounds

By the Numbers

FRAME SIZES & AMOUNT OF HONEY IT CAN HOLD

- Deep = 19 inches x 1-1/16 inches x 9-1/8 inches = 6 Pounds Honey
- Medium = 19 inches x 1-1/16 inches x 6-1/4 inches = 4 Pounds Honey
- Shallow = 19 inches x 1-1/16 inches x 5-3/8 inches = 3 Pounds Honey

HONEY PER 10 FRAME BOX

A shallow super will typically yield between 25 and 30 pounds of honey or 2 to 2 ½ gallons.

A medium (6 5/8") depth super will typically yield between 35 and 40 pounds or 3 to 4 gallons.

A full-depth box will typically yield between 60 and 70 pounds or 5 to 6 gallons.

HONEY VOLUME = WEIGHT

- 1 Gallon Honey = 12 Pounds
- 1 Quart Honey = 3 Pounds
- 1 Pint Honey = 1.5 Pounds
- ½ Pint Honey = 12 Ounces

Choose wisely!

2

GRADUATING FROM A BEEHAVER TO A BEEKEEPER

You can no longer keep bees like Grandfather kept bees!

Almost anybody can keep bees on their property nowadays and when they die all they must do is go and purchase some more. Everybody is selling bees these days all you must do is use Google and type the search as shown to the right and ad in the quotation marks “Honeybees for sale”.

When your Honeybee colony, or maybe just the queen, dies they will gladly sell you more!!

To me it is no surprise but you may find everyone from the local beekeeper, the big name feed store, Walmart and others may be offering Honey Bees for sale and they are even willing to ship them to your door from almost anywhere across the country, If you are willing to pay the price.

What everyone should be truly concerned with is that vast number of new and old BeeHavers who can't seem to KEEP their honeybees alive from year to year today. The producers of package honeybees have surely learned what is needed to keep honeybees alive and healthy, or they would be in some other line of work today. BeeHavers must accept that they need to change their present management techniques, if they truly have any. They must have the desire to learn and GRADUATE from a BeeHAVER to a beeKEEPER!

I started beekeeping at the age of 23 and knew nothing about what I was getting into. I obtained my first colony, 2 Deeps and 1 medium super, and hauled them home in the back of my 1984 Ford Ranger. I tied them down and I do not even remember blocking off the entrance to the hive, but it was dark when I went to pick them up, so I am sure I was ok. I placed them behind the house right next to a small metal storage building and I could see them when I walked out the back door. They were placed in a shady spot that allowed them to get great morning sun but after noon the sunlight was diffused by a large tree that grew in that area.

For a few mornings that I did not have to work I would go set on a concrete block, that I had placed beside that hive, and just set and watch as the girls went about their duties. I was amazed at how hard they worked and understood that not a one of them in that hive did anything for themselves. Everything they were doing was for the sake of the whole colony.

I asked around when I could to find other beekeepers in the

town I lived in and did find a couple of beekeepers in the country that I could go visit as well as an attorney who kept honeybees that I could go visit on weekends but by appointment only. I had to make sure he had free time to discuss honeybees. I am not talking about a time he was doing nothing I am talking about times when I knew he was not going to charge me for his time. He never did but that was the way I saw it at the time.

As I spent this time with these beekeeper's I quickly realized I had gotten into something that many wanted to but few were willing to dedicate the time to learn to do it properly. This was not something to just go at it haphazardly or fly by the seat of your pants. Neither was it something that took all your time 24/7.

There were things that needed to be done at specific times of the year as well as when specific things were happening inside of your hive. Back then we had much fewer diseases, pests and parasites that seems as if they were created just to devastate your honeybee colonies.

I did get my colony through their first winter with me and even collected honey from that colony in year number 2. I cut the comb from the frames and put some of it in jars. Then squeezed the honey out of the remaining comb into those jars on top of the comb and poured what remained into jars that did not include comb. I then put the left-over comb with honey left in it into a large pan and put it into the oven at a very low temperature and overnight the wax melted and separated from the honey. I poured the extra honey into their own jars but used the warm wax to pour on top of each of the jars I was planning on giving away.

. . .

When the wax had cooled it left an approximate ¼" wax seal in the jar on top of the honey. I then screwed on the lids and stored that honey away. I think I may have had less than 24 pints of honey stored away that I was proud give to others and tell them that it came from the bees I had. If you notice I did not say I was keeping bees but instead I was right, I had bees.

That second year I did my first cutout for free. It was in the inside corner on the back side of a home that had a large window on the left side that joined the wall that had the honeybees inside. It was on the other side of town from where I lived but I did go to visit the homeowner to see what they had. I truly do not remember how they contacted me, but it must have been on the phone that hung on the wall as no one I knew even had let along know what a cell phone might be.

When I arrived, we talked about what he had, and he took me around the house to the area and I could see the wall was stained from where the honeybees were inside. I told him I could get the honeybees out, though I had never done so before, but that I would make no repairs to the home. I let him know that I would be as gentle as possible when disassembling that area, the honeybees were occupying.

When we had an agreement, well I do not think he had a choice as the wife wanted those bees gone out of her home at whatever the cost.

After I got home my brother-in-law and I rounded up a few items that I thought we needed, we typically spent time together on weekends doing guy stuff anyways but looking back at it now, I think it was just what his sister did to keep an eye on me.

When we got back to the home that we were about to dissect the bro-in-law had on long pants and a long sleeve shirt and there I stood in my cutoff jean shorts and a T-shirt. You know, Professional Beekeeping Gear! I do not remember having but 1 veil and 1 pair of beekeeper's gloves and I am sure that he was the one wearing those. I did have my smoker ready to go prior to removing the first board from the Masonite lap siding of that home. I could see the honeybees were entering at the top of the wall so that is where I was smoking. After all of the siding was removed for over 12 feet down that wall, we could see the seams in the plywood on the walls.

I took my tiny crowbar and my hive tool and began to remove the first section of plywood and was amazed that there in front of me from the top to the bottom of the cavity and in a total of 4 sections, that we at least 18" on center, of that wall was a massive gob of comb and honeybees. They were everywhere and there I stood in my cutoff jean shorts and t-shirt and tennis shoes with no socks. I do not remember getting stung one time though I remember laughing quite a bit at the brother-in-law dancing around with bees in his shirts and pants, go figure.

Now again us being professionals all I had brought to take the honeybees home in were cardboard boxes. I was smart enough to bring a roll of screen to place over the boxes and tape into place as it was needed.

I remember we had 3 boxes full of honeybees and I did locate 3 queens, one for each box. I had cut out the comb in sections large enough to set nicely inside of those cardboard boxes and when I though I had done all the damage I could do we left with me giving my word to the homeowner that I would return before daylight the next day to assess the situation.

I made it home successfully with my new bees and after contacting my beekeeping buddies I let them know the stupid thing I had just done but they each assured me that they would be over the next morning, luckily that was Sunday, after church and help me out.

I went back to the home before daybreak the next day and found that we had left very few stragglers in those walls. I wish I knew now how I had accomplished that. I do not remember receiving any stings during any of this adventure and again have no clue how that was possible or if I was just too young and dumb to be concerned with it.

A little after 9:00 am, on Sunday, my first buddy arrived and after I showed him what I had and discussed what I had found and done, 1 queen per cardboard box, he smiled, got back into his truck and left. He said nothing else but was just gone. I thought this may not be a good sign.

Maybe 30 minutes later my second buddy arrived with 2 deep boxes, bottom boards, inner and outer covers, and frames for each of the boxes. How did he know what to bring?

Approximately 15 minutes later my other friend returned and in his vehicle was the beekeeping lawyer as well. Now at this age I did not know if this was a good thing or not. Then they all got out of the vehicles and he also had a couple of complete hive setups and I was sort of relieved though still concerned.

I later found out how tight a true beekeeping community could be because when the first friend had gotten home, he had called the other two and they had a game plan way before they ever arrived. When all was said and done, I now was the proud beeHaver of 4 colonies of honeybees. I owed them nothing for the gear nor for the time they took out of their day to help a young beeHaver grow his apiary. One colony I kept on my property where it set for over 12 years before we sold that place and moved out into the country. I moved it to some land that I had purchased in another county and had then for many more years. The others I had moved out to the country onto a friend's property which he took over and I never kept tabs on them.

Yes, I had re-queened that colony a few times through the years and harvest plenty of honey from them. More importantly I began to pay more attention on my forays to visit the fellow beekeepers that had helped me that day. They taught me quite a bit as I grew but the one thing that I walked away with and still try to remind myself today.

The honeybees have ben doing honeybee stuff for millions of years. I can try to manipulate what they are doing to try to assist it what they are doing but, in the end, they will always know more about being honeybees than I or anyone else will ever know. It was the things in those early years that my friends and fellow beekeepers taught me that to this day I to try to get the new BeeHavers to understand what I am saying when I answer a lot of their questions with just a few words, "Think Like a Honeybee" that is what I try to do any time I am interacting with a colony trying to understand why they are doing what they are.

Remember too, **"Think Like a Honeybee"!**

3

INTRODUCTION TO HONEYBEES

The honeybee is an incredible insect. Honeybees produce honey, the world's most popular sweetener. Honeybees also play a vital role in pollinating many of the world's crops. In this chapter, we will explore more about honeybees, why they are so important, and how we can help them.

HONEYBEES ARE the most well-known of the bees that produce honey. They are social insects and live in colonies. Each colony can have up to 80,000 bees. Honeybees have six legs, four wings, three body parts (head, thorax, and abdomen) and two compound eyes.

HONEYBEES FEED on nectar and pollen. The nectar they collect is regurgitated and turned into honey. This is the sweet substance that adorns the shelves of our supermarkets. The pollen they collect is used to feed the larvae and to create the wax comb. This comb is used to store the honey, pollen, and eggs. The honeybee also has a sting, which is used to defend the colony.

. . .

Honeybees are very important for humans. They are vital for the pollination of many of our crops. Their pollination has been estimated to be worth $14.6 billion to U.S. agriculture every year. Honeybees are also a symbol of many cultures. They are mentioned in many religious texts and are used as a symbol for many celebrations.

However, honeybees are in danger. There are many threats to their populations. These include pesticides, disease, habitat loss, climate change and parasites. We must do our part to help preserve these important insects. We can do this by planting wildflowers, creating bee-friendly habitats, limiting use of pesticides, and spreading awareness of the importance of honeybees.

Honeybees have been a part of our world for many thousands of years and they are essential for the future of our environment and our food supply. By learning more about them and doing our part to help, we can ensure that honeybees remain a vital part of our world.

4

SOURCES FOR PURCHASING HONEYBEES

When it comes to purchasing honeybees, there are a variety of sources available to beekeepers. Before buying, it is important to consider the type and quality of bees, the cost, and the potential risks associated with the purchase. Here, we will discuss the different sources available and how to select the best one for you.

1. **Local Honeybee Breeders** – Local beekeepers who raise and sell honeybees can be one of the best sources to purchase quality bees. As they are more familiar with the characteristics of their bee colonies, beekeepers know which colonies are particularly good for pollination, producing honey, or producing queens. They can also advise you on the most cost-effective option.

2. **Purchasing Online** – There are a number of websites where honeybees can be purchased online. These sites offer various types of bees, such as nucs, packages, queens, and even liquid bees. However, buying from an unknown seller or from another

country may be associated with some risk, as there is no way to ensure quality or originality.

3. **Beekeeping Supply Stores** - Beekeeping supply stores provide a variety of honeybees and related supplies.When buying from a supply store, ask about the quality of the bees, the cost and any warranties the store offers on their products.

4. **Bee Breeders' Associations** – Many countries have bee breeders' associations, which work to protect and improve bee breeding and provide precision breeding across countries. These associations can be a good source of information on quality bee breeders and recommended sources of bees.

5. **Swarms** – Another way to obtain honeybees is to capture swarms, which can be a challenging but rewarding experience. Capturing swarms can also be a great way to buy bees at no cost.

Whichever source you choose, make sure to do your research. Consider the type of bees, cost, and quality as well as the potential risks associated with the purchase. Once you have made your decision, it's time to get to work on establishing your own hive!

5

THE PROS AND CONS OF RAISING HONEYBEES

The idea of buying a package of honeybees to raise and keep as a hobby can be appealing to many. The prospect of helping the environment and having a source of homegrown honey adds to the allure of buying honeybee packages. While the rewards that come with keeping honeybees may outweigh the risks for certain individuals, it's important to weigh the pros and cons before making the decision to buy a package of honeybees.

Pro: Local Pollination

One of the biggest benefits of keeping honeybees is providing local pollination for your area. Honeybees are essential for the health of our environment as they pollinate much of the flowers, fruits, and vegetables that grow in our gardens and farms. Without them, many of these plants would not produce food, thus reducing the available food sources for both humans and animals. As a beekeeper, you'll be able to help your local environment and make sure that other species nearby are receiving the needed pollination.

. . .

Con: Bee-Related Health Concerns

For people in good health, handling honeybees and their associated materials should be fine. However, it's important to be aware of the health risks that come with being a beekeeper. Stings are one risk that everyone should consider before purchasing honeybee packages. Sting victims may experience an allergic reaction that could be fatal if not treated immediately. Additionally, various diseases can be spread from bee to bee and even to the beekeeper. It's important to educate yourself on aerially transmitted diseases and wear protective clothing at all times when handling bees.

Pro: Homegrown Honey

Honeybees produce honey from their nectar gathering from plants and flowers in their environment. For those with a sweet tooth, honey produced from their own bees can be immensely satisfying, not to mention the cost savings. It's a great feeling knowing that your bees are playing a role in benefiting not only your own diet but that of your family and friends.

Con: Beekeeping Cost and Maintenance

Though more affordable initially, purchasing honeybee packages is the beginng cost of beekeeping, and there are others, including protective clothing and equipment such as hive boxes and queen cages. Not to mention the required upkeep of their environment, such as feeding, managing diseases, and providing protection from predators. All of these monthly costs combined with the general cost of the bees should be taken into consideration when deciding whether or not to purchase honeybees.

. . .

In conclusion, there are both pros and cons to purchasing honeybee packages. While there may be more risks involved than rewards for some, for those in good health and willing to take the time and money to maintain their bees, the rewards can be considerable. Compassion for the environment combined with a source of homegrown honey can make for a rewarding hobby and experience.

6

ROLES OF HONEYBEES

Honeybees carry out several roles in a colony, which help in the overall functioning of the organization.

The Queen Bee:

The queen bee is the matriarch of the colony and plays a critical role in its functioning. She is producing the eggs which will become the worker bees / drones within the hive. She is responsible for the reproductive cycle of the colony, and she also has the ability to secrete pheromones which help to create an organized system within the colony.

The Worker Bees:

The worker bees are the backbone of the colony and are responsible for a variety of tasks. They take on many roles including care of the queen, foraging for nectar and pollen, building beeswax comb for the storage of food, tending to the brood, and defending the hive. Worker bees are all female and live for around 6 weeks.

The Drones:

The drones are the male bees in the colony and play a less important role than the queen or worker bees. Their main purpose is to mate with new queens from other bee colonies and their lifespans usually do not exceed 6 weeks.

The Role of Honeybees in Pollination

Honeybees play a critical role in the pollination of flowers, fruits, and vegetables. The worker bees collect nectar and pollen from flowers and bring it back to the hive where it is used to make honey. As they fly from flower to flower, they help to spread the pollen and help ensure the reproduction of plants.

The Role of Honeybees in Honey Production

Honeybees also play an important role in the production of honey. They collect the nectar and pollen, bring it back to the hive where it is stored in beeswax comb. The worker bees then use their saliva to convert the nectar into honey and store it for future use. Honey is an important source of food for people around the world.

The Role of Honeybees in Balancing the Ecosystem

Honeybees also help to maintain the balance in the ecosystem. They help to pollinate varieties of plants which provide vital nutrients for the surrounding environment. They also help to protect plants from pests and can even help to reduce the spread of disease by physically preventing some pests from getting close to the plants. In short, honeybees help to support overall biodiversity in an ecosystem.

Conclusion

Honeybees play an incredibly important role in the functioning of a colony. From the queen bees who orchestrate the reproductive cycle, to the worker bees who gather food and take care of the brood, to the drones who ensure the health of the population, honeybees are essential to the health of a hive and to the general ecosystem.

7

QUEEN HONEYBEES

Queen honeybees do not rule the colony but it is instead the other way around.

The queen is nothing more than an egg laying machine that the others allow to live as long she works out for the good of the colony.

THERE ARE many reasons a colony may kill their queen:

- She is damaged
- Egg laying rates are declining
- Her pheromones have diminished
- Something is wrong with the brood she lays
- Hive stress

THERE ARE a multitude of reasons that we are not aware of but they do what they feel is best for the colony as a whole.

8

LIFE CYCLE OF A QUEEN HONEYBEE

The life cycle of the queen honeybee is an interesting and complex process that is essential to the success of the colony.

THE QUEEN IS responsible for the production of all the worker bees, drones, and future queens.

SHE HAS a unique purpose and set of roles that she needs to fulfill for the colony to survive and prosper. In this chapter, we will look at the queen honeybee's life cycle from the egg stage to her death.

Egg Stage

Once the queen is mated and has left the colony she will lay about 1,500 to 2,000 eggs a day in the hive. These eggs are fertilized and she will lay them singularly into sealed wax cells. As each egg hatches, it enters the larvae stage of development.

Larvae Stage

During the larvae stage the newly hatched larvae will be surrounded by worker bees who will attend to them. These worker bees will feed them a special diet that is specifically designed to stimulate their growth. As the larvae grow and become larger, drone bees will be added to the mix to help feed them. The queen can live up to five years in this stage.

. . .

Pupae Stage

The larvae will then enter the pupae stage, where they will encase themselves in silky threads and transform into adults. During this stage, they will be nurtured by the worker and drone bees while they transform. This process can take up to three weeks.

Adult Stage

Once the bee has emerged from its cocoon, it is now an adult. The new bee will then be released from the hive and the cycle begins again. During this stage, the bee will become a forager and venture out in search of nectar and pollen for the colony. It is also responsible for the defense of the hive, as well as construction.

Death

The life of the queen honeybee typically ends when she is killed by one of her own offspring. This can happen when she is unable to lay enough eggs or when a newly mated queen takes over. The average queen can live between two to five years.

Conclusion

The life cycle of the queen honeybee is long and complex and essential for the success of her colony. She must go through various stages of growth and development before emerging as a fully formed adult. The new bee will then be responsible for the egg laying and health of the hive, as well as the defense and construction of the hive. Once the queen is unable to lay eggs or has been replaced by another queen, she will sadly meet her untimely end.

9

WORKER HONEYBEES

The aptly named worker honeybee is a crucial member of any honeybee colony. Worker honeybees are female bees and responsible for a wide range of tasks to ensure the colony's success and longevity.

THE MOST IMPORTANT task for the worker honeybee is foraging for food. Worker honeybees leave the hive and search for flower blooms to collect nectar. To locate flowers, the bees rely heavily on their sense of smell and sight. Some bees may also travel up to 2 miles away from the nest to find food. Once the flower bloom is located, the worker honeybee uses her long proboscis to lap up nectar and store it in the crop, or second stomach. The nectar is then converted into honey, which is the main source of food for the honeybee colony.

THE WORKER HONEYBEE is also responsible for building, protecting, and maintaining the beehive. When the worker honeybee is not out foraging, they are at home inside the hive. Worker honeybees collect wax to build honeycomb and use their wings to fan the hive and maintain a consistent temperature. They also guard the hive and protect it from predators.

WORKER HONEYBEES PLAY an important role in the rearing of young bees. Worker honeybees help queen bees to keep the hive populated and ensure the colony's success. Worker honeybees feed the queen bee and hatchling larvae and ensure that the environment of the hive is favorable for rearing and nesting. In addition to caring for the young, worker honeybees also place a duty on collecting and storing pollen. With their furry legs, the bees collect and store pollens which contain proteins and other essential nutrients for the colony.

OVERALL, the worker honeybee is an integral member of the colony and does a great job at work. Without the diligent efforts of these essential workers, the honeybee colony would not feel successful.

THE WORKER HONEYBEE is a vital member of the bee colony. A worker bee is a female bee whose primary purpose is to collect nectar and pollen from flowers, and then turn the nectar into honey. Worker bees also build the hive, care for the young bees, defend the hive, and clean the hive. They are the most numerous and active bees in the colony and are essential for the hive's survival.

WORKER HONEYBEES BECOME active over the spring, when the hive awakens from its winter slumber and the flowers begin to bloom.

During this time, the worker bees start searching for food, which is mainly nectar and pollen. When they find a food source, they fly back to the hive with the goods and deposit them into the honeycomb. The nectar is then turned into honey through a process that involves the bees fanning their wings over the food to evaporate the water content.

Worker bees also play a key role in caring for the growing brood inside the hive. As the young bees hatch, the worker bees feed them and ensure that the hive remains clean and organized. Since the workers are all female, they cannot reproduce and pass on their genes; however, they are still valuable members of the hive, as they help to build up the bee population.

The worker honeybee is an essential part of the bee colony, as it plays a crucial role in the hive's health and nutrition. Without the dedicated work of the worker bee, the bee colony would not be able to survive. For all of their hard work, the worker bee deserves recognition and appreciation.

10

LIFE CYCLE OF A WORKER HONEYBEE

Honeybees live in highly organized colonies and work together in harmony. While the entire colony plays an important role in the functioning of the hive, the worker honeybees are the most crucial for the survival and success of the colony. Worker honeybees go through a well-defined life cycle, starting as an egg and culminating in their ultimate demise.

Stage 1: Egg

The worker bee's life begins with the queen bee laying an egg. The egg hatches into a small larva after a few days of incubation.

Stage 2: Larva

The larva goes through three stages of life: the larvae stage (1st–6th instar). During this time, worker bees care for the larvae as they consume food supplied by the colony. As the larvae mature, they eventually spin their cells with wax and then remain in a pupal state.

. . .

Stage 3: Pupa

The pupal stage lasts 12–16 days. During this time, the pupae develop the physical characteristics of a worker bee, including wings, eyes, and legs.

Stage 4: Immature Worker Bee

The pupae develop into adults known as immature worker bees. These bees are responsible for foraging for nectar and pollen as well as building and tending to the hive. Since immature worker bees cannot mate, they only have a short lifespan consisting of around a month before they eventually die from exhaustion or become too old to work.

Stage 5: Mature Worker Bee

Mature worker bees are responsible for foraging and gathering food for the colony. In addition to foraging and nursing, mature worker bees also take on jobs such as hive cleaning and comb building. Mature worker bees live for around 6 weeks before they eventually die of exhaustion or become too old to work.

Stage 6: Death

The life cycle of the worker honeybee ultimately culminates in death. Worker honeybees typically die in the field, due to predators and disease, or in the hive, due to exhaustion.

In conclusion:

The worker honeybee life cycle is an important part of the colony's success. Worker honeybees start as eggs and mature into adults, performing crucial roles within the hive until they eventually die. The worker honeybee's life is ultimately short yet essential for the continued survival and success of the colony.

11

SCOUT HONEYBEES

The honeybee colony contains a variety of different roles, and each of them is important. The scout honeybees are responsible for finding and evaluating food sources, and they are vital.

SCOUT HONEYBEES FLY out of the hive to search for potential sources of nectar or pollen. This can be done anywhere within three miles of the hive but usually takes place within a one-mile radius. Once they find a good source, they mark the spot with their hind legs and a pheromone signal, which other bees can then follow to that same location.

THE SCOUT BEES THEN EVALUATE the potential food source. They assess the quality of the pollen and nectar, and this includes assessing the sweetness of the nectar, the number of flowers in the area, and the plant species from which the nectar comes from. All of this information is communicated back to the hive through a complex system of dances and chemical signals.

. . .

Once a good source of food is identified, scout bees will begin to recruit other worker bees to go and collect the food. They do this by performing specific waggle dances which guide other bees to the location. The recruits will then go and gather the food, and the scout bee will remain in the area to ensure other sources of food are not overlooked.

Scout honeybees are essential for the survival of the colony. Without them, the other bees would have no way of knowing where the best sources of food were located, and the survival of the hive would be greatly diminished.

12

FORAGER HONEYBEES

The forager honey bee is an essential piece of the beekeeping puzzle. Each beekeeper needs these bees in order to harvest honey and to pollinate. The forager bee is the first in line and is the most important honey bee in the hive.

THE FORAGER HONEYBEE'S main job is to collect both nectar and pollen from flowers. This is done by hovering in front of a flower and using its proboscis, which is a tongue-like organ, to suck up the nectar. It then deposits the pollen on its back legs and carries it with it to the next flower. Once it has been loaded up with nectar and pollen, the forager honeybee returns to the hive.

They have important grooming and communication skills, which they use to keep the hive in shape and in communication. The forager bees also do the job of carrying the nectar and pollen back to the hive, making them hardworking and vitally important to the success of the hive.

. . .

THE FORAGER LIFE cycle is deeply rooted in the hive's production of honey. Foragers are typically born into the community and start working at around a month old. When the forager is born it begins to specialize in the task that it will do as it moves from one month to the next. As each forager matures, it works to learn more about its role in the hive production.

WHEN A FORAGER IS ready to start its job, it heads out to the field to collect nectar and pollen from flowers. The forager will fly from flower to flower, collecting the nectar and pollen until its sac is full. It then returns to the hive, where the nectar and pollen are put in the hive's storage.

FORAGERS PLAY an important role in the hive's survival because they make sure that the hive has plenty of food and pollen to survive off of. Therefore, it is important that beekeepers have plenty of forages around the hive so that they can produce the honey the beekeeper needs.

WITHOUT THE FORAGER BEES, beekeepers would have to work hard to make sure that their hives had enough food. Therefore, the foragers are an essential part of beekeeping that beekeepers depend on to keep their hives producing the honey they need.

13

NURSE HONEYBEES

Nurse honeybees are an important part of the colony and play an integral role in the health of the hive. Nurse honeybees are unequivocally female, and they are the youngest bees in a colony. Nurse honeybees take care of the larvae, clean the cells, feed the queen bee and other adult bees, and make wax comb.

Nurse honeybees go through a few stages as they mature. During the first stage, they are known as "nurse bees" and they feed the larvae with a mixture of regurgitated nectar and pollen. This mixture is known as "bee bread" and it provides the essential nutrition for the larvae to grow and develop.

In the second stage, nurse honeybees switch over to becoming "house bees". House bees' responsibilities involve cleaning, building comb, and helping to guide new members of the hive. They are also in charge of taking temperature readings within the hive, making sure the temperature is stable.

. . .

As they enter the third phase, nurse honeybees begin to switch over to being "foraging bees". These bees are the ones you see outside, buzzing around flowers collecting nectar and pollen to bring back to the hive. Foraging bees are the most important type of bee in the hive because they are responsible for collecting food for the colony.

Nurse honeybees are highly essential for the health and stability of the hive. Without their help, the colony will not last. Therefore, it is important to make sure that nurse honeybees are as healthy and strong as possible so that the entire hive benefits.

14

DRONE HONEYBEES

In a honeybee colony, the drones are the male bees. These are the male bees charged with the task of mating with the queen to ensure the continuation of the species. Unlike the worker bees, the drones lack stingers, therefore they are one of the few bee types that humans can safely handle. Drone honeybees play an important role in the colony, as they are responsible for cross-pollination, which is essential for plant health and the production of honey.

THE LIFE CYCLE of the drone honeybee begins when the queen lays an egg in a special cell that is bigger and more elongated than the ones used for worker bees. This egg will then hatch and the larva will be fed royal jelly and pollen until it reaches the pupa stage. After this, the drone will emerge as an adult and begin its mission of mating with the queen.

THE DRONES' bodies are adapted for mating, being longer and heavier than worker bees. Drones have large eyes that help them locate and recognize the queen, better enabling them to mate with her. Additionally, the drones' larger wings allow them to fly more quickly and accurately so they can reach the queen.

DESPITE THEIR IMPORTANCE TO CROSS-POLLINATION, Drone honeybees are typically expelled from colonies in the fall. The worker bees know that the drones will not be able to provide food once winter arrives, thus they remove the drones from the hive in order to save resources. During "drift" season, entire colonies of drones will gather near hives, waiting to find a new queen and colony to join when warmer weather arrives.

THE LIVES of Drone honeybees may be short, but their importance to the overall health of the colony, and to the environment, cannot be understated. The efforts of these bees should be appreciated and safeguarded.

15

LIFE CYCLE OF A DRONE HONEYBEE

Drones are a type of honeybee that play a vital role in the honeybee hive. They are sexually mature male honeybees responsible for mating with the queen. To carry out this task, they go through a rather unique lifecycle compared to the other types of honeybees. Understanding this lifecycle is essential to appreciating this species and its vital role for the survival of the colony.

THE LIFECYCLE of a drone honeybee begins with the queen bee laying a fertilized egg. This egg will develop into a male honeybee, more specifically a drone. The hatchling will look similar to adult worker honeybees and begin to develop more distinctive physical characteristics as they get older. As they continue to grow, they will become larger, longer, and more hairy than the workers. They will also have large, pronounced eyes that give them excellent vision. As they grow up, they will be able to fly and feed themselves.

. . .

At this stage, the drone will be ready to mate with the queen. For this to happen, the drones will first scout the area and look out for queen bees in search of a mate. When they find one, they will form a nuptial flight with other drones. The drones will then take part in a mating "game"; where competing drones will jostle for a chance to mate with the queen. The strongest and fittest drone is successful in mating and the queen will store his sperm in special sacs for future use.

After mating, the drone will no longer be necessary. This means its lifespan has already come to an end and it will die soon after. As the drone is no longer needed, it is kicked out of the hive, reducing the amount of food the colony has to provide to its members.

Although drones do not live long, they are indispensable to the colony and its lifecycle. By providing the queen with new genetics, they ensure that the health and strength of the colony continues. Furthermore, their brief existence helps to make sure the hive remains at an optimal size. By understanding the lifecycle of the drones, we can be amazed by the beauty and fragility of honeybee colonies.

16

HONEYBEE FOODS

Honeybees need a variety of foods to keep them healthy and productive. A bee colony depends on pollen and nectar to provide nutrition and to stimulate brood production. In order to meet the nutritional needs of a busy hive, beekeepers must be proactive in providing a steady supply of diverse high-quality foods.

Pollen: Bees collect pollen from flowers and store it in wax combs. This provides essential protein and some fats and vitamins. Pollen is used to feed the queen and young larvae, and it is the primary source of food for other adult bees.

Nectar: Nectar is a sugary fluid secreted by flowers and collects on the outside of the flower's petals. Bees collect this sweet substance, transfer it to the hive, and then process it into honey. Nectar is the energy source for the adult bees.

. . .

Honey: Some honey is used to feed the queen and the young larvae, but most of it is stored as food for the hive and for future use. Honey is high in sugar and provides energy when other dietary sources are scarce.

Water: Honeybees consume water for their own hydration and to help absorb nutrients, cool down the hive, and mix food.

Beekeepers must provide a variety of foods for their bees. This is especially important during times of low nectar flow. Prepared pollen substitutes, liquid sugar solutions, and candy boards are excellent supplemental foods for honeybees during these periods of stress.

By providing high-quality foods, beekeepers can ensure that their bees stay healthy, productive, and well-fed. With the right combination of nutritious, diverse foods, honeybees can thrive.

17

POLLEN

Honeybees make use of pollen in several ways. Pollen is important for the overall health of the honeybee colony and is used for a variety of purposes.

First and foremost, pollen is used as a source of food for the adult worker bees. Worker bees bring back the pollen from foraging trips and store it in the hive. It is then broken down and included in a mixture called "beeswax," which the worker bees consume as their main source of energy.

When the workers return from foraging, they eat the stored pollen to replenish their spent energy. In addition to providing energy for the workers, pollen provides vitamins, minerals, and proteins for the growth and development of the colony.

THE HONEYBEE COLONY also uses pollen to produce honey. During the honey-making process, nectar that has been collected is regurgitated and broken down within the honeybee's stomach. In order to break down the nectar, enzymes are added to the mix, and these enzymes come from the pollen that the honeybees have brought back from their foraging trips. The pollen also helps to thicken the honey, giving it a smoother, more spreadable consistency.

LASTLY, pollen also helps the honeybee colony to expand. The pollen that is brought back to the hive is used by the queen bee to fertilize the eggs that she lays. Fertilized eggs will eventually become new adult worker bees, meaning that the hive can grow larger and more populous. New members of the hive will then help to carry out important functions within the colony, such as pollinating flowers and gathering nectar and pollen.

IN CONCLUSION, pollen is a vital component of the honeybee colony, and it is used for a variety of purposes. It provides energy for the worker bees, helps to create honey, and facilitates growth in the colony by allowing eggs to be fertilized. Without pollen, the honeybee colony would collapse, thus illustrating the importance of this tiny but mighty substance to the success of the honeybee.

18

NECTAR

Nectar is a natural sweet liquid produced by flowers and used by honeybees to make honey. Honeybees require nectar to help sustain their colony and to feed their young. Honeybees use nectar to make honey, which is their primary food source.

When a honeybee finds a flower with nectar, it visits the flower multiple times to sip the nectar and carry it back to the hive in its honey stomach. The nectar is digested in the honey stomach, and the useful components are used to make honey.

Honeybees also use nectar to make "bee bread," which is a mix of pollen and nectar that is fed to the larval stage of honeybees. When the larval stage is complete, they become adult worker bees.

Nectar is also important for the pollination process. When a honeybee drinks the nectar, some of the nectar gets stuck on their eyes and other body parts. As they fly around, they bring the nectar to other flowers and help to distribute pollen and other nutrients needed for plants to reproduce.

In addition, nectar can help honeybees regulate the temperature of their hive. During the warmer summer months, they use the sugar in the nectar to evaporate water and cool the hive down to more comfortable levels.

In short, nectar is an essential part of a honeybee's lifestyle and helps them to sustain their colony and make honey, bee bread, and provide important pollination services. Without nectar, honeybees would have trouble surviving.

19

WATER

Water is very important to a honeybee colony and will seek out sources of water which could include your neighbors pool

HONEYBEES NEED WATER for several reasons.

WATER IS NECESSARY FOR HYDRATION, as well as for regulating their body temperatures, for gathering nectar and for reducing the risk of diseases.

As pollinators, honeybees need water to help them survive and water is a high priority for them.

HERE ARE some of the ways that honeybees use water:

1. **Hydration:** Water is essential to the functioning of honeybees and their general well-being. As temperatures rise and they're exposed to the sun, they need water to keep their bodies cool, as well as maintain their metabolic rate and energy levels.

2. **Pollen Collection:** Honeybees need water to help collect and hold the pollen grains together when they're working in the field. They also use water to help pull the nectar out of flowers and dilute it for easier transport back to the hive.

3. **Disease Prevention:** Water is used by honeybees to help prevent diseases from spreading within the colony. By drinking the water from the pond, river or bird bath, honeybees can help flush out infected bacteria or parasites in their system, reducing the chances of the disease spreading.

4. **Regulating humidity:** Controlling humidity within the hive: Honeybees use water to regulate the relative humidity in their environment. This is just as important as keeping it cool in the summer.

WATER IS a critical resource for honeybees and is essential for their ability to forage, pollinate and ultimately, survive.

ON HOT DRY DAYS, they can require more than a quart of water just for temperature control!

IN THE HEAT of summer it is used for evaporative cooling.

BEES NEED water to dilute stored honey. Honeybees **can not** consume crystalized honey or sugar without water.

NURSE BEES CONSUME large amounts of pollen, nectar, and water so that they can produce royal jelly which is used to feed the larvae.

FEED LARVAE - A larvae diet can consist of 80 percent water during the first day of growth and about 55 percent on the sixth day.

WHAT WE MAY CONSIDER AS dirty water has a better chance of attracting a bee than sparkling water straight from the spigot. Honeybees seem to be more attracted to water that smells like wet earth, moss, aquatic plants, worms, decomposition, or even chlorine.

20

BEE BREAD

Bee bread is an important, special mixture of honey, pollen, and bee secretions that serves as a primary food source for a honeybee colony.

BEE POLLEN, also known as bee bread and ambrosia:

BEE POLLEN with added honey and bee secretions, made and stored in brood cells by forager bees, and used as food for worker bees and larvae.

IT PROVIDES the bees with essential proteins, carbohydrates, vitamins, and minerals and is made in a complex process that involves the collective efforts of multiple bees in the colony.

. . .

The process of making bee bread begins with a bee gathering pollen from plants. The bee will land on a flower and use specially-adapted hairs on its body to collect pollen grains.

After the bee has gathered a load of pollen, it will bring the load back to the hive where other bees will mix it with honey and special enzymes and secretions produced by the bees themselves.

The mixture is then compacted into a rich wax called bee bread, a substance that has the same texture and color of regular bread, but is more nutritious and holds more vitamins and minerals.

Bee bread is a key food source for the bees—it is the primary source of carbohydrates and proteins and is essential for their overall health and development. As larvae and young bees, the bee bread provides essential proteins and carbohydrates that helps their growth and development. Older bees, too, rely on the bee bread for its energy and vitamins that are essential for maintaining their health and strength. Bee bread is especially important in winter months and times of scarce food, when it is the only source of nutrition available to the colony.

Bee bread is an important, complex, and integral part of a honeybee colony. Not only important for its nutritional value, the collective effort of multiple bees and the meticulous process of producing it creates a bond within the colony that reinforces the overall strength and health of the community.

21

HONEY

Honeybees need honey for a variety of purposes.

Honey bees collect nectar and pollen to make their sweet food for survival and is mainly utilized in the winter months. Honeybees in fact produce honey, beeswax, propolis and royal jelly.

Honey bees make honey as a way of storing food. Honey provides a source of energy for the hive, which in turn helps the bees maintain their health.

Honey is full of nutrients and is a great energy food, because it is high in sugars

. . .

Honey bees convert the sweet nectar they gather from flowers into honey which they store in the cells of their honeycomb.

The nectar that they collect has a high water content and it must be condensed or concentrated to the correct water to sugar ratios prior to the honeybees capping the cell it is stored in. Bacteria and fungi cannot multiply in high concentrations of sugar, and this is why honey rarely goes bad.

Honey is food the bees can store and eat during the winter months, or when there is little other food sources available, during a death for example.

The honey you are familiar with, is made by honey bees. Bumble bees and wasps don't make honey. Though Bumblebees do create and store little pots of nectar.

Honey is used to feed the hive's larvae, as well as store pollen, nectar, and wax in the form of beebread. Beebread is an incredibly important source of nourishment for the bees, as it provides a wide range of nutrients and minerals that keep them healthy and functioning properly.

Honey also serves as an important resource for the hive, as bees use it when waxing and building the honeycomb in their nest. The honeycomb is used to store food and also provides additional protection and insulation within the hive.

22

ROYAL JELLY

The role of royal jelly, also called Bee Milk, in honeybee life is an important one. Honeybees use royal jelly in a variety of ways, most notably during larval development and the development of QUEENS.

Royal jelly is fed to all larvae in the colony, regardless of sex or caste.

Royal jelly is secreted from the glands in the heads of worker bees and is fed to all bee larvae, whether they are destined to become drones (males), workers (sterile females), or queens (fertile females).

After three days, the drone and worker larvae are no longer fed with royal jelly, but queen larvae continue to be fed this special substance throughout their development.

. . .

ROYAL JELLY IS essential for bee reproduction. During the creation of a new queen bee, the bee larvae are fed a concentrated diet of royal jelly.

This unique diet allows the new queen to grow to a much larger size and gives her the capacity to lay a larger number of eggs than her workers. Royal jelly also keeps her safely anchored to the roof of the structure, called a queen cell, in which she develops.

HONEYBEE LARVAE WILL ONLY DEVELOP into queen bees when they are fed large quantities of royal jelly.

ROYAL JELLY IS 67% water, 12.5% protein, 11% simple sugars, and other trace minerals

ROYAL JELLY IS KNOWN to be involved in communication between adult and larvae. Adult workers secrete and exchange important chemical signals with larvae via royal jelly.

These chemical signals help to keep the colony functioning smoothly by informing larvae of potential danger and helping them to find essential food sources.

23

THE HONEYBEE AND PROPOLIS

Honeybees are an essential part of the world's ecosystem. As pollinators, they play an integral role in nature's cycle of life. Their work does not stop there because honeybees also produce a number of other vital products for human use. Propolis is among them.

Propolis is a wax-like resinous material that bees use to coat the internal surfaces of their hive. It's a naturally occurring substance produced by honeybees as they gather materials from a tree's sap and resin. The bees mix the substances with a variation of things like pollen, wax, and saliva to create the sticky yet rock-hard protective coating within their colonies.

From the researches and studies, it is clear that Propolis is essential for the well-being of honeybee colonies. It has a number of positive benefits for the hive, such as repelling predators, protecting the colony against disease, and providing a protective barrier against weather elements.

. . .

PROPOLIS IS ALSO beneficial to humans. Its anti-inflammatory and anti-microbial properties make it a common ingredient in natural remedies. Propolis is said to aid with things like easing skin ailments, such as warts and cold sores, while its use in mouthwash and throat lozenges helps to promote oral health.

MORE THAN ANYTHING, the collection of propolis by bees ensures the protection and continuation of their colonies—a service that we inherently enjoy and benefit from. Honeybees as a species, and propolis as a substance, provide essential benefits to humans and the natural world in general. It is for this reason that propolis is so valued, and the honeybee's role in the production of this powerful substance should not be overlooked.

PROPOLIS, often referred to as "bee glue" or "bee gum," is a resinous material collected by honey bees from the sticky buds of certain trees. This sticky substance is used by worker bees to construct, maintain and protect the hive. After leaving the hive to forage for nectar and pollen, bees will transport a small amount of propolis on their front legs and use it for various hive related tasks.

PROPOLIS IS MOST COMMONLY USED by honeybees to line the interior of the hive, especially the cracks and crevices around the hive entrance, to form a protective barrier from wind, rain, and other environmental elements. Worker bees apply propolis in thin layers and heat their bodies to soften and spread the propolis so that it forms a tight seal. This sealant helps to keep out small hive pests, such as mites, as well as large predators, such as bears.

. . .

HONEYBEES ALSO UTILIZE propolis in the creation of cells and combs, providing structural reinforcement and stability. This helps to ensure that cells and combs can endure the regular vibrations of the hive while protecting the nectar and honey stored within.

PROPOLIS IS ALSO a crucial part of the hive's ventilation system. Worker bees, by simultaneously adding and removing propolis, maintain the interior of the hive at a temperature that is most optimal for hive health and productivity.

FINALLY, honeybees use propolis to reduce the bees in the hive, by blocking the scent trails of young bees leading back to the hive. This helps to prevent robbing, a behavior in which bees from another colony enter the hive and steal honey or pollen.

24

PURCHASING LOCAL HONEYBEES

Pros of Purchasing Local Honeybees

1. **Supporting Local Apiaries:** Purchasing locally produced honeybees is a great way to support local apiaries and their important work. Supporting a local business has many environmental and economic benefits that contribute to the health of your local community.

2. **Quality Control:** Apiaries that sell locally produced honeybees use high-quality queen bees and robust colonies. Local beekeepers understand the importance of maintaining strong and healthy colonies, and local honeybee products are often held to a higher standard than those imported from other countries. This ensures that you are supporting sustainable and ethical beekeeping practices.

Now do not assume this is true as when it comes to most of the Local Queens you may be offered to buy, the so called beekeeper knows nothing about grafting queens and instead will offer to sell you what ever queen that may be available in one of their hives at the time you need a queen. Get something in writing guaranteeing her age and genetics. Do not be afraid to spend the money and have her tested if she dies. Many offer open bred queens that they have no way of knowing what she was bred with on her maiden flight!!!

. . .

3. Varietal Diversity: Honeybee colonies come in different varieties, each with their own unique qualities. Purchasing local honeybees also ensures that you are getting a diverse range of bees with different traits, catering to any special needs you may have. They are true HYBRIDS and unless artificially inseminated there is no way to know the genetics, or traits of the offspring until they populate a colony.

4.Freshness: Local honeybees are sold directly from the hive and into your hands. This means they are always fresh and ready to produce delicious honey that is rich in flavor. You can possibly see them before you buy them.

Cons of Purchasing Local Honeybees

1. Price: Buying local honeybees can be more expensive than importing them from another location. This is because local beekeepers have to spend more money to produce high-quality bee products, and there is also the added cost of transportation. Truly there is no reason for the extra cost.

2. Limited Variety: Local beekeepers often have a limited selection of bee varieties, meaning that if you are seeking a specific type of bee you might have to look elsewhere for a better selection. Unless they artificially inseminate them they are selling HYBRIDS

3. Seasonality: Beekeeping is a seasonal activity, so local apiaries can be closed or limited in honeybees during certain times of year. This means that if you need to buy honeybees during the offseason you'll have to look elsewhere. Most do not care after the fact and will sell anyone colonies of bees at any time in any conditions. Then when they die they will gladly sell you more.

. . .

4. **Disease:** Local honeybees can sometimes carry diseases and pests, which is why it's important to do your research before purchasing. Make sure that the apiary you purchase from takes regular preventative measures to keep their colonies healthy and productive. Always ask for proof they have been inspected.

5. Many, but not all beekeepers that you may find on the Internet, YouTube, TikTok, Instagram, Twitter etc... and the list goes on are more interested in the viewer numbers so that they can get free gear from business offering their wars. They know that if you see them using it then there are good odds you will purchase those items. None of them truly have your intentions at the front of there minds and to them it is only $$$$. Most will not share their real contact details with their followers as they do not want to be bothered unless you want to pay to come to one of the shows they are being paid to speak at.

Ask them and see how many will tell you what they may be paid to speak at functions, did they comp a free meal, travel, food, products to review? These are all forms of payment and be sure to ask them what is the NEW things that they are bringing to the world of beekeeping?

Maybe they speak better or have more appeal in front of the camera but there is nothing new, that in my opinion, 95% of them have to offer.

Ask them to send you a few free queens, split you off colonies, provide you free hardware like hive components and even protective gear and see what you get.

Oh a discount may seem good but ask for it for free. Tell them to give you their address and you will swing by to pick it up. You will find there are very few of us that do any of that any more.

25

PROS AND CONS OF BUYING HONEYBEE PACKAGES

Pros of Buying Honeybee Packages:

1. Cost – Honeybee packages tend to be cheaper than buying a Nuc, as they may be more readily available and offer a better deal for purchasing multiple colonies.

2. Brood Comb – Honeybee packages generally come with several frames of already established brood comb, giving the new hive an instant boost of activity and resources.

3. Variety – Honeybee packages can be custom sourced from multiple apiaries and have a greater variety of queens and genetics from which to choose.

. . .

Cons of Buying Honeybee Packages:

1. Limited Stress Tolerance – Honeybee packages have a lower threshold for stress, as they are not used to living in a confined environment before arriving to their new hive.

2. Poor Leadership – Honeybee packages lack the natural instincts that a Nuc possess in developing a successful, productive colony.

3. Disease Risk – Package bees have a greater risk of carrying and transmitting diseases, particularly if they were not raised in a healthy environment.

26

PROS AND CONS OF BUYING A HONEYBEE NUC

Pros of purchasing Honey Bee NUCS

1. Versatility. A nuc (also known as a nucleus colony) can be an ideal choice for a beginner because it comes fully established with a queen, workers, brood, and honey stores already in a frame. This means they can be used to start a completely new colony or to replenish an existing one. It can also be used as a way to start a number of colonies in a very short span of time.

2. Ease of use. Since the nuc is typically in a wood or plastic box, it is much easier to quickly unpack and place into its own hive body or directly onto an existing one. This is especially useful for those who don't have the time or desire to construct their own hive from start to finish.

. . .

3. Quality assurance. Buying a nuc can also be helpful in terms of quality assurance. It is much easier to ensure that the nuc is healthy before introducing them to an existing colon

CONS of purchasing Hone Bee NUCS

1. Price. A nuc may cost up to twice as much money as a package of honeybees, making them a much more expensive investment.

2. More risk. As with any package of bees, there is always the risk of them being of poor quality. Since the nuc is already established, it is much harder to tell if the bees are healthy before purchasing.

3. Take longer. Nucs cannot just be dropped into a hive like a package of bees can. This means it can take significantly longer to get the colony up and running. This can be especially challenging for beginning beekeepers.

27

PURCHASING A NUC OF HONEYBEES COMPARED TO A PACKAGE OF HONEYBEES

When it comes to getting started as a beekeeper, one of the biggest decisions you'll have to make is whether to purchase a Nuc or a Package of honeybees. Both have their advantages and disadvantages, so it helps to understand the differences between the two.

A Nuc is short for nucleus. It is a box containing an established colony of honeybees that are already living in a hive. This established colony has its own queen, workers, and other essential components needed to survive and produce honey. The cost of a nuc varies, but it's generally more expensive than a package of honeybees.

On the other hand, a package of bees is a sealed box of 3-6 lbs of adult honeybees with a queen that needs to be installed in a hive. With this type of colony, the bees will have to create a new hive structure and build combs from scratch. The cost of a package of bees is much less than a Nuc.

. . .

When deciding between purchasing a Nuc of honeybees and a package of bees, there are a few things to consider. First, how much time and effort do you have to commit to beekeeping? A package of bees requires a lot more work and dedication to establish a hive than a Nuc does as the bees will have to create their own hives and combs from scratch. A Nuc provides a more established structure and can get to producing honey quicker than a package of bees.

Another important factor to consider when purchasing honeybees is the cost. A Nuc is usually more expensive than a package of bees, but the cost of supplies and tools needed to create a hive for a package of bees may cost almost as much as the Nuc. Additionally, the amount of time needed to get a package of bees thriving and producing honey can be a lot more than with a Nuc as it can take up to 8 weeks for a package of bees to begin producing nectar and collecting pollen.

In conclusion, when it comes to purchasing honeybees, there is no right or wrong answer. It comes down to personal preference, budget, and the amount of time and effort you are willing to commit to the task. A Nuc provides a more established colony with a queen and a hive structure that is ready to begin producing honey quickly, while a package of bees requires more work and dedication to get started but offers a cost-saving choice for those getting started in beekeeping. Ultimately, it's a personal decision, and it's important to take the time to weigh the advantages and disadvantages of each when choosing the best option for you.

28

RAISING YOUR OWN QUEEN HONEYBEES

As anyone who keeps honeybees knows, the health of a colony depends heavily on its queen. Unfortunately, a honeybee colony can experience a queen failure after a few years, so many beekeepers choose to raise their own queens to ensure a healthy hive. There are several different ways to raise a new queen honeybee.

The two most common methods of queen rearing are grafting and open mating. In the grafting method, worker brood is grafted from a healthy hive into artificial queen cells. After the queen larvae are developed, these cells are placed with a nucleus colony. A nucleus colony is a small colony created from a full-sized hive with the intent to raise a queen bee. The nucleus colony houses the transplanted brood and helps to raise a new queen.

Open mating is another method for raising a queen bee. To use this method, beekeepers must have two hives, one with a laying queen and one nucleus colony. The nucleus colony is then taken to a spot where there are other queen bees flying. You should provide a feeder on the nucleus hive to provide sustenance for the new queen to ensure she has enough energy to fly. Once she has mated, the beekeeper installs her in the other hive and monitors her to ensure she is laying.

REGARDLESS OF THE METHOD USED, raising a queen bee requires a certain degree of experience and training. Aspiring beekeepers should do plenty of research and practice before attempting to rear their own queens. Join a local bee club or follow other veteran beekeepers to gain valuable information and advice. Furthermore, it helps to have the right equipment on hand. Tools such as queen traps, grafting tools, and cages help make the queen rearing process easier.

RAISING a queen honeybee is a complex process and should not be attempted by a novice. With the right training and equipment, however, it's possible to raise numerous high-quality queen bees from one hive. By doing so, you can ensure your colonies stay healthy and productive for years to come.

29

GRAFTING HONEYBEE QUEENS

Grafting queen honey bees is a skillful practice that allows beekeepers to produce large amounts of queens quickly. This can greatly increase the efficiency of a queen producing operation.

However, it should be done with care, as a grafter must be highly knowledgeable to ensure the health and well-being of the bees.

In this chapter we will go over the basics of grafting queen honeybees and provide some tips to ensure success.

Step 1: Collecting the Grafts

This is the first step in grafting queen honeybees. It can be done any time during the queen-rearing process, but it is best to do it no later than the day of mating or one day after the mating flight. To collect the grafts, you will need a hive board or other type of substrate in which to place the bees that were collected from the mating colony. The board should be placed near the entrance of the mating colony and tweaked slightly until the bees start congregating beneath it. Bees will then stick to the board and can then be collected into a container.

Step 2: Preparing the Grafts

Once you have collected enough grafts, you can begin to prepare them for grafting. This is done by gently blowing on each graft in order to loosen up the pupae, then gently rubbing them until they roll up into a tight ball. This process allows you to transfer the pupae from the board to the grafted frame. The process should not take too long but can be time consuming if you have a lot of grafts to prepare.

Step 3: Grafting the Grafts

When the grafts have been prepared, they can now be grafted onto the frame. This is done by carefully picking up each graft and placing it into a cell of the grafted frame. The cells must be the correct size and depth for the queen pupae, and the cells should have a bit of space after the graft has been placed in. This helps to ensure that the pupae do not get overcrowded.

Step 4: Incubating the Grafts

. . .

The next step is to incubate the grafted frames with the queen pupae. This is done by placing the grafted frame into an incubator box. The box should be maintained at the correct humidity and temperature, and should be kept free of any external drafts. The box should also be properly sealed to ensure maximum efficiency.

Conclusion

Grafting queen honeybees is a skillful practice that, when done correctly, can greatly increase the efficiency of a queen-rearing operation. It is important to follow the above steps carefully in order to ensure success. With practice, it is possible to become a skilled grafter and help to increase the queen-producing efficiency of your beekeeping operation.

30

CREATING AN INCUBATOR BOX FOR QUEEN GRAFTING

Queen grafting is an important part of beekeeping, as it allows beekeepers to increase hive population and introduce new genes into their population.

However, it is important to ensure that the resulting queens are healthy and strong. This is where the incubator box for queen grafting comes in. Queen grafting requires an incubator box to control temperature and air circulation, both of which can have a significant impact on the health and development of queens. Creating an incubator box is an important step for ensuring successful queen grafting.

First and foremost, it is important to ensure that the box is well insulated to maintain an optimal temperature. Most suitable boxes are made from Styrofoam with a lid, as this will provide good insulation while still allowing access to the queens while they are in their incubation process. It is important to make sure the lid is placed securely, as any drafts will disturb the consistent air-temperature during the incubation process.

The box should also be placed in an area of the apiary that has access to sunlight and good air movement, as both these factors will reduce the possibility of cool draughts and can help the queens stay healthy during the incubation period. Additionally, the box should be placed away from direct sunlight, to prevent overheating.

The box should also be equipped with a thermometer, as this will enable up to date readings of the temperature inside the box and allow beekeepers to make adjustments if necessary. This is especially important as the incubator box requires a specific temperature (approximately 90-95 degrees Fahrenheit) for successful queen grafting. Additionally, the box should have a fan to provide airflow, as this will ensure the temperature is spread evenly.

Once the incubator box is prepared and the queens placed inside, the incubation process can begin. The queens will remain inside the box until they emerge as adults approximately seven days later. During this period, the box should not be opened, as the sudden change in temperature, and disruption of airflow, can negatively affect the development of the queens.

Once the queens have emerged, the incubator box should be removed from the apiary in order to prevent any disruption of climate, which could lead to damage in the bees. After this, the incubator box is ready to be used for future queen grafted batches.

. . .

IN CONCLUSION, the creation of an incubator box for queen grafting is an important step for ensuring the health of new queens. The box should be made from Styrofoam and have a lid, be placed in an area of the apiary with access to sunlight and good air movement, have a thermometer and fan, and have the box removed from the apiary once the queens have emerged. An incubator box will help provide the necessary conditions for successful queen grafting.

31

CELL STARTERS FOR QUEEN REARING

In a cell starter, nurse bees initiate queen rearing when grafted cell cups are introduced to a colony that is queenless, and absent of queen cells and young larvae.

WHEN BUILDING a cell starter colony it is best to introduce frames of closed brood only as any viable eggs or larvae of the right age may be utilized by the queen less colony that you are building to raise their own queen.

This may divert resources away from your grafts, and create undesired emergency queen cells. The grafted cells provided by you should the only source of young larvae in the colony.

One way to create a cell starter is to create a new queenless colony by shaking nurse bees into a Nuc. A single frame of open brood is added to the center of the Nuc and with 2 frames on each side containing pollen and nectar. If needed one of the outer frames can be replaced with a frame feeder. Better yet would be a rapid feeder utilized to feed the colony from the top so as not to have the need to disturb the colony any more than needed.

Shake in as many nurse bees as you can get to fit inside of the box and even best to where you feel it can hold no more. Any field bees will return to the original box but the nurse bees will stay in their new colony to care for the brood frame.

Cell starters with more nurse bees and food resources can raise more queen cells.

A few hours to one day after the starter colony is assembled, it will be ready to receive grafts. The grafting frame is exchanged with the single brood frame in the starter colony.

Nurse bees will begin caring for the grafted cells immediately. If needed, the started cells can be viewed the following day by gently brushing the nurse bees from the cells and looking at the contents from below.

Caution! Do not shake or invert the grafting bar; the young larvae are delicate and susceptible to drowning.

Cells should be partially drawn and have a pool of royal jelly in the center with the larva visible, sitting on top of the royal jelly.

After the cell starter is prepped and at least 24 hours prior to grafting and placing your grafted cells into your starter, shake as many nurse bees as you can fit into it. if there are any field bees that get shaken in they will fly back to the colonies they came from.

Remove the top center frame just prior to introducing your frame of grafted cells, more if you have more frames but I like one frame per cell starter setup, and replace the top on the starter.

You can peak in a few days if you must but just remember the time-frame of a queen bee being born.

A queen emerges 16 days after the egg was laid, or 13 days after the egg hatches into a larva. If a larva 24 hours old is grafted, a young queen will emerge 12 days later.

5 frame Nuc with super for Cell Starter

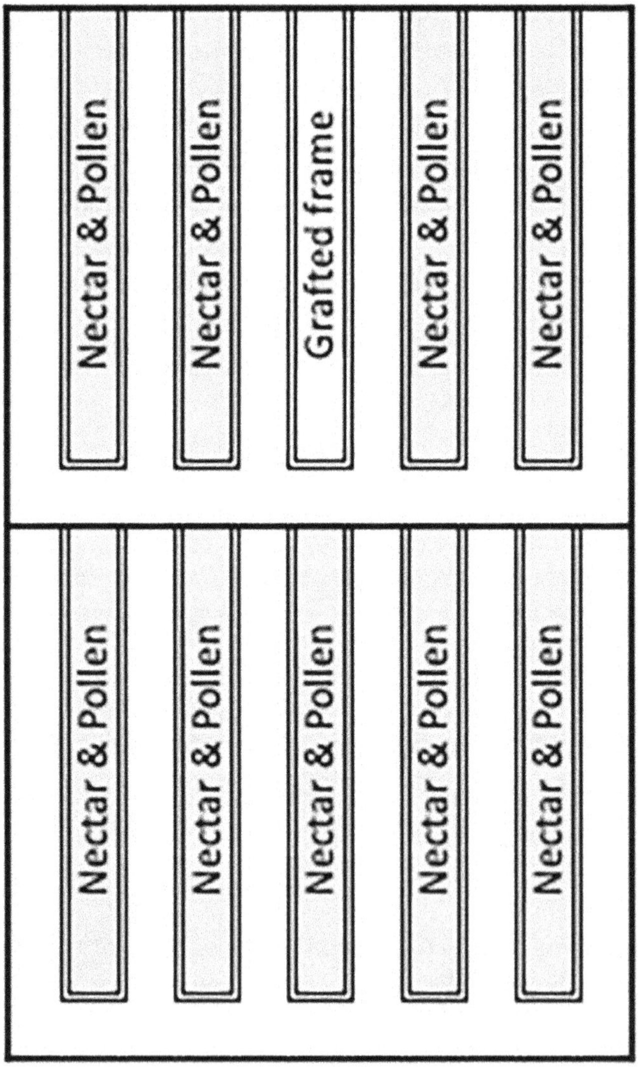

Nectar & Pollen
Nectar & Pollen
Grafted frame
Nectar & Pollen
Nectar & Pollen

Nectar & Pollen
Nectar & Pollen
Nectar & Pollen
Nectar & Pollen
Nectar & Pollen

32

CELL FINISHERS FOR QUEEN REARING

If you plan to use the same colony to start and finish queen cells. The queen, frames with young brood, and some workers are temporarily removed from the colony. This leaves the remaining colony in a queenless state.

YOUR GRAFTS CAN BE PLACED in this colony any time from four hours to one day after the queen has been removed. After the grafted larvae are introduced it is possible to use this colony to finish building the queen cells.

~

QUEENLESS CELL FINISHERS are typically converted into Nucs after a single use because the behaviors that allow for productive rearing diminish with extended periods of without a queen.

If you wish, you can reunite the colony with the original queen. Since it has been queenless for a maximum of two days they should readily accept their original queen. If you are going to do this a queen excluder needs to be placed between hive bodies and the queen is confined to the lower portion of the hive, while the grafted cells remain above the queen excluder.

IF YOU ARE USING a separate cell finisher, the cell bar is carefully moved to the awaiting colony.

The Queenright cell finisher colony feeds and builds the started queen cells.

Nurse bees must be abundant to care for the developing queens, while vast numbers of foragers must be available to feed and sustain the nurse bees.

Cell builders are most commonly made from colonies that occupy two deep hive bodies, but they can also be made with mediums or Nucs. A queen excluder must be utilized to ensure the queen is trapped in the lower hive body.

Make sure there is no queen or queen cells above the queen excluder. Any queen who exists or emerges above the excluder will kill all of the grafted queens

Regular assessment must be made of your cell finisher as they are held at a state of ready to swarm at any time. They require regular assessment and intervention by the beekeeper.

Colonies with younger queens are less likely to swarm and they are more prolific layers. Nectar, pollen and brood frames in the finisher may be exchanged with other colonies to maintain a constant state of growth. Sugar syrup, along with fresh pollen or pollen patties, should be freely available and replenished regularly.

5 frame Nuc with super
for Cell FInisher

Nectar & Pollen
Nectar & Pollen
Grafted Frame
Nectar & Pollen
Nectar & Pollen

Queen Excluder

Nectar & Pollen
Brood
Queen
Brood
Brood
Nectar & Pollen

33

TRAITS WANTED FOR HONEYBEES

Hygienic Behavior

Hygienic behavior is probably the most successful achievement in breeding bees. It's been very well studied and proven to be effective against chalkbrood, American foulbrood, and varroa.

Brood Viability

Temperament

Tracheal Mite Resistance

Resistance to tracheal mites has recently been found to be a grooming behavior. The bees use their middle legs to groom the mites away from their tracheal opening.

Grooming behavior as the mites migrate from one bee to another could be a means of control. This trait appears to be controlled by dominant gene(s) and occurs widely in honey bees.

. . .

Honey Production

High honey production results from the right number of healthy bees being in the hive at the proper time.

Comb Building

They may belong to the same species, but you can select the right breed for you according to certain characteristics, such as the following:

Docility.
Tendency to swarm.
Timing of brooding.
Suitability to the local climate.
Disease resistance.
Honey production.
Propolis production.
Winter-coping abilities.

Learn to raise your own queens and you will have much more control of the items mentioned above.

Never be afraid to look for sources of wild honeybees that may have survived a few years in a tree or other cavity. You do not have cut them out but seek them as a source for swarms or places to hang your swarm traps.

You will not get better local bees than bees that are truly local to the area!

34

QUEEN HONEYBEE MATING

Honey bee queens mate in flight with numerous drones from diverse genetic sources.

SEASONAL EFFECTS INFLUENCE the timing of natural mating. Spring reared queens tend to mate more efficiently and be- gin compared to fall reared queens.

THE TECHNIQUE of instrumental (artificial) insemination provides a method of complete genetic control and with improvements in instrumentation, the technique is highly repeatable and highly successful.

INSTRUMENTAL INSEMINATION also enables the creation of specific crosses that do not occur naturally, providing significant advantages to research and stock improvement.

A single drone can be mated to one or several queens, isolating and amplifying a specific trait

The ability to combine sperm cells from hundreds of drones and inseminate a portion to a queen or batch of queens enables unique mating system designs and simplifies stock maintenance.

Virgin queens have a brief, optimal receptive period for mating. The age queens typically take mating flights is between 4 and 13 days post-emergence. Virgin queens older than 14 days tend to mate with fewer drones and store fewer sperm cells.

Virgin queens can be instrumentally inseminated when they are a few days to several months old. However age will affect their performance.

35

PROS AND CONS OF NATURALLY BRED HONEYBEE QUEENS

Naturally inseminated honeybee queens are more readily available and can be found in the majority of the Apiaries but even more importantly, in the wild.

Naturally Mated Queens will vary in the genetic makeup of their offspring based on the genetics of the drones that may be flying in the area that the queens may visit on their mating flights.

For artificially inseminated queens there is no need for mating flights.

Pros of Naturally Bred Honeybee Queens

1. Better Taste: Naturally bred queens tend to be in closer contact with nature, and the honey gathered from these queens is said to have a more natural flavor.

. . .

2. Reduced Pesticide Presence: As naturally bred queens live and forage in more natural conditions, there is a lesser presence of pesticides and other chemicals which can be detrimental for human consumption.

3. Increased Disease and Parasite Resistance: These queens tend to have a better immunity and natural resistance to different diseases, as well as being more resistant to various parasites.

4. More Vigorous Brood: Naturally bred queens tend to possess a more vigorous brood, and their offspring is generally healthier and longer lasting compared to those propagated with artificial queen rearing methods.

Cons of Naturally Bred Honeybee Queens

1. Cost: As raising queens in a natural environment requires more effort, skill, and time compared to artificial rearing, the cost for these queens are often higher than for those propagated with artificial methods.

2. Risk of Inbreeding: The risk of inbreeding is very high due to the limited gene pool available in a natural environment. This can increase the chances of problems regarding disease resistance and the overall strength of the hive. An open mated queen will mate

with approximately 15 drone honeybees, all of which may potentially be from unknown origins.

3. Poor Proximity to Apiaries: As naturally bred queens are often far away from the apiaries, they may not adapt as quickly to their new environment.

4. Time-Consuming: As selecting the right queen requires a lot of time and observation, it can be a laborious task that may not produce the desired results.

5. Risk of the queen being lost: There are a number of reasons a queen may not return from her mating flight and those do include just getting lost and even becoming someone else's meal.

36

PROS AND CONS OF ARTIFICIALLY INSEMINATED HONEYBEE QUEENS

Instrumental (artificial) insemination of queens is a skill that takes time and practice to master

The actual insemination process is quick and easy.

- Queens are put to sleep with CO_2.
- Under a low power microscope the queen is positioned in the insemination device.
- The stinger is gently pulled out of the way and the syringe inserted.
- 8 micro liters of semen injected into the oviducts and the sperm will migrate to the spermatheca.

Artificially inseminated honeybee queens are gaining in popularity, with more beekeepers turning to this method in order to produce queens of a reliable and high-quality.

. . .

THE ADVANTAGE of a breeder queen versus an open-mated queen is that maternal AND paternal lines that are 100% known and carefully identified

WHILE THE PROCESS is relatively easy, there are some pros and cons associated with the practice. In this chapter, we will explore both the pros and cons of artificially inseminated honeybee queens.

Pros

1. Accuracy – Artificial insemination of honeybees allows for the queen bee to mate with a carefully chosen and precise drone, thus providing more control over the breeding process and decreasing the possibility of mating with weaker or inferior drones.

2. Increased Genetic Diversity – With artificially inseminated queens, beekeepers can use multiple drones for the insemination process, whereas natural queen bees will typically only mate with one drone. This enhances genetic diversity and can lead to more resilient bee populations. A breeder queen has been specifically bred, selected, and inseminated for genetic excellence.

3. Quality Assurance – Due to the precise and calculated nature of the process, beekeepers can be sure that they're receiving high quality queens that will be better suited for production and better suited to tackle the challenges they may face in their environment.

Note: *Queens can be mated to a single drone, simplifying selection for specific traits or Queens can be mated to hundreds of drones, maintaining genetic diversity.*

Cons

1. Cost – Artificially inseminated queens come with additional costs. Not only do beekeepers have to pay for the semen of the chosen drone, but they also need to purchase specialist equipment, as well as someone experienced in carrying out the insemination process correctly.

2. Femicidal Tendency – Some species of drones, such as the Stingless Bees, have a tendency to attack and kill the queen after insemination, due to the presence of semen from other drones. This can have a negative impact on queen production and queen longevity.

3. Risky Process – Artificial insemination is a risky process and can often result in the death of the queen if it's not carried out properly and with extreme precision.

4. Artificially insemination is very useful to fix genetic traits fast and cheap but it neglects natural selection on drone quality. Successful mating with a queen in the field requires drone health to be optimal, Hence - Survival of the fittest

Conclusion

Overall, there are both pros and cons associated with artificially inseminated queen bees. While the process may provide greater accuracy and quality assurance, it's also a costly and potentially risky venture. Beekeepers must weigh up the pros and cons and decide which benefits outweigh the potential disadvantages before investing in this practice.

37

REARING DRONE HONEYBEES

Drone rearing is just as important as queen rearing.

MANY NEW AND even more experienced beekeepers may consider DRONES as worthless to their colonies.

QUEENS CAN BE RAISED ALMOST ANYTIME but without a viable quantity and genetic diversity of DRONES with can be a limiting factor in Late Season as well as Early Season Queen Production.

38

HONEYBEE SWARMS

Bees are known for working hard and producing large amounts of honey and other forms of food for humans. However, when honeybee colonies get to be too large, a process called swarming can begin. A honeybee swarm is when the colony divides in two and half of the workers and a queen fly away to find another place to start a new colony.

When a bee colony decides to swarm, it is a sign that the colony has become overcrowded within the current hive structure. The process of swarming happens when the queen bee leaves the original bee colony with half of its workers in a search for a new home.

The honeybee hive also splits in two, with the other half of the worker bees staying in the original colony to care for the remaining queen and young.

One of the most interesting parts of the honeybee swarm is the dance of the scout bees. Before the swarm leaves, bees will send out scouts to search for a suitable new home. The scouts communicate their findings with other bees by performing a waggle dance. In this dance, the scout describes where the new home will be located, and the other bees follow the directions to their new home.

When a swarm is about to settle in for a new home, they generally form a cluster on a tree or other structure. This is when professional beekeepers may come in and create a managed colony using the bees of the swarm.

For those that are interested in beekeeping, honeybee swarms can be an exciting part of the process. Since a honeybees swarm contains half of its population and its queen, it is the perfect sized to start a managed hives. If a colony nearby is going through a swarm, those interested in beekeeping may contact a local honeybee organization to provide assistance in capturing the swarm and starting a managed hive.

Honeybee swarms may be looked at as a destructive and worrisome process, but it is an essential part of the honeybee life cycle. For many, honeybee swarms can be seen as an amazing experience that should be taken in and appreciated.

www.ingramcontent.com/pod-product-compliance
Lightning Source LLC
Chambersburg PA
CBHW050557301025
34739CB00021B/344
* 9 7 9 8 8 5 3 2 5 2 5 6 1 *